Co⟍

The Book ⟍ ⟍ation

by Stratford Caldecott

All booklets are published thanks to the
generous support of the members of the
Catholic Truth Society

CATHOLIC TRUTH SOCIETY
PUBLISHERS TO THE HOLY SEE

Contents

Introduction

The Book of Revelation, or *Apocalypse* (from the Greek word meaning the "lifting of a veil"), describes itself as the Revelation of (or from) Jesus Christ, sent through an angel to the Apostle John. What is unveiled by it may be Jesus Christ himself, or a series of events that "must soon take place," or the mysteries of the kingdom of God - perhaps all three things at once. But it remains a deeply puzzling and confusing text for most people. Often we scan through it quickly, catching only the main images - a Woman clothed with the sun, a Dragon, the Four Horsemen, Babylon, the Heavenly City - not stopping to absorb the rest, or ponder their spiritual meaning. But "He who has an ear, let him hear what the Spirit says to the churches," says John (*Rv* 2:17). This little book is written to help the non-specialist reader to "hear" what the Spirit is saying to us in the last book of the Christian Bible (last in order of arrangement, but perhaps among the first to be written).

Revelation in popular culture

A lot of Christians, mostly Evangelical, take the Book of Revelation very literally. The influence of Hal Lindsey's 1970 book *The Late Great Planet Earth* has been enormous, as has the multi-million selling *Left Behind* series of novels by Tim LaHaye and Jerry Jenkins, which describes the rise of a charismatic European leader who turns out to be the Antichrist, leading to the battle of Armageddon in northern Israel, Christ's thousand-year reign with the saints, then the final confrontation with Satan, the destruction of the old earth and the descent of a new world from heaven. The Russian philosopher Vladimir Solovyev (d. 1900) wrote a famous short story about the Antichrist that follows a similar pattern.

Several Catholic novelists in the twentieth century, including Robert Hugh Benson (*Lord of the World* and *Dawn of All*) and more recently Michael O'Brien (*Father Elijah*), have contributed to the genre. The figure of the Antichrist in these stories is inspired partly by the Book of Revelation and partly by Saint Paul's references to the future coming of a "man of lawlessness", a "son of perdition, who opposes and exalts himself against every so-called god or object of worship, so that he takes his seat in the temple of God, proclaiming himself to be God" (2 *Th* 2:3-12). Pope Saint Pius X drew attention to this prophecy in 1903, connecting it with the modern tendency to substitute man for God, the "distinguishing mark of Antichrist," and subsequent Popes have warned of the dangers of secularism, consumerism and relativism - though without necessarily indicating that all these dangers will be rolled together in one man.

Understanding Revelation

Jesus reminds us in Matthew 24:36 that "of that day and hour no one knows, not even the angels of heaven, not the Son, but the Father only." It is also very clear from everything we know about the ancient near eastern peoples, and the internal evidence of the Bible itself, that many of the images and prophecies which abound in Scripture were intended to be read as symbols and similes, not as literalistic predictions. So the wisest thing to do is not to get carried away by people saying "There he is!" or by the wars and rumours of wars that seem to presage the end (*Mt* 24:6, 23). The end may not be as nigh as you think!

Who was John? The traditional view identified him with the "disciple whom Jesus loved," supposedly the author of the fourth Gospel. That would make him the son of the fisherman Zebedee, one of the two "sons of thunder" (see *Mk* 3:17), an Evangelist and member of the Twelve, who had known Jesus personally on earth. *This* John is said to have lived to be a very old man (*Jn* 21:20-24), looking after the Virgin Mary, the Lord's own mother (*Jn* 19:26-7), until her assumption into heaven, and had written his Apocalypse possibly in exile on the Aegean island of Patmos some time before his death towards the end of the first century. From as early as the third century, however, biblical scholars have doubted this identification, and the truth is that we do not know who the author really was. This book will not concern itself further with the question, since we are more interested in what the book says than who wrote it down.

Pope John Paul II gave us an example of how to interpret the Book of Revelation as applied to our own times in his Apostolic Exhortation, *Ecclesia in Europa* (2003). In the beginning of this document he wrote as follows:

> The Book of Revelation sets before us a word addressed to Christian communities, enabling them to interpret and experience their place in history, with all its questions and its tribulations, in the light of the definitive victory of the Lamb who was slain and who rose from the dead. At the same time, it sets before us a word which calls on us to live in a way which rejects the recurring temptation to construct the city of man apart from God or even in opposition to him. For should this ever happen, human society itself would sooner or later meet with irreversible failure.
>
> The Book of Revelation contains a word of encouragement addressed to believers: beyond all appearances, and even if its effects are not yet seen, the victory of Christ has already taken place and is final. This in turn causes us to approach human situations and events with an attitude of fundamental trust, born of faith in the Risen One, present and at work in history.

Pope Benedict XVI echoes his predecessor in the General Audience of 23rd August 2006 (published by CTS in the booklet *Christ and His Church*). There he writes that the "Seer of Patmos" wants to tell us:

> trust in Jesus, do not be afraid of the opposing powers, of persecution! The wounded and dead Lamb is victorious! Follow the Lamb Jesus, entrust yourselves to Jesus, take his path! Even if in this world he is only a Lamb who appears weak, it is he who triumphs!

> The subject of one of the most important visions of the Book of Revelation is this Lamb in the act of opening a scroll, previously closed with seven seals that no one had been able to break open. John is even shown in tears, for he finds no one worthy of opening the scroll or reading it (cf. *Rv* 5:4).

> History remains indecipherable, incomprehensible. No one can read it. Perhaps John's weeping before the mystery of a history so obscure expresses the Asian Churches' dismay at God's silence in the face of the persecutions to which they were exposed at that time.

> It is a dismay that can clearly mirror our consternation in the face of the serious difficulties, mis-

understandings and hostility that the Church also suffers today in various parts of the world.

These are trials that the Church does not of course deserve, just as Jesus himself did not deserve his torture. However, they reveal both the wickedness of man, when he abandons himself to the promptings of evil, and also the superior ordering of events on God's part.

Well then, only the sacrificed Lamb can open the sealed scroll and reveal its content, give meaning to this history that so often seems senseless. He alone can draw from it instructions and teachings for the life of Christians, to whom his victory over death brings the message and guarantee of victory that they too will undoubtedly obtain. The whole of the vividly imaginative language that John uses aims to offer this consolation.

It is in this spirit that we should try to read the Book of Revelation today.

The Book of Revelation as a whole

The structure of the book

Revelation opens with John on Patmos being commissioned by God to send a letter to the seven churches in Asia (the introductory verses 4-8 form a kind of executive summary of the whole book). After this prologue, the book unfolds in six or seven main sections, followed by an epilogue to balance the prologue. However, the complexity of the text that we find sandwiched between this prologue and epilogue cannot be overestimated. Whichever way we choose to divide it, there will be repetitions, overlaps, reversals of chronological order, and multiple perspectives on the same events described in different metaphors, as well as numerical patterns both on the surface and hidden in the depth of the text.

It helps to notice first that the Apocalypse falls naturally into a simple structure of *two main parts*, with the second part beginning at chapter 12 (this is the chapter that shows us the famous vision of the woman clothed with the sun and crowned with twelve stars). The following summary is based on an outline by Ian Boxall:

Ch. 1:1-8. Prologue and opening. (Christ the Alpha and Omega.)

Part I. Preparation of the Church and the opening of the Lamb's scroll.

Ch. 1:9-3.22. Inaugural vision and the seven messages to the churches.

Ch. 4:1-8:1. Throne vision and the seven seals of the Lamb's scroll.

Ch. 8:2-11:19. Seven trumpets.

Part II. Unveiling of the Lamb's scroll and visions of the Church

Ch. 12:1-15:4. Seven visions.

Ch. 15:5-19.10. Seven bowl-plagues.

Ch. 19:11-22:11. Seven final visions of the Church.

Ch. 22:12-21. Epilogue. (Christ the Alpha and Omega.)

Numbers and their significance

In what follows we will work through these sections in detail, becoming more aware of the images, and the order in which they have been placed, and their possible meaning. But before we do so it might be worth saying something about *numbers* in the Book of Revelation. The Seer of Patmos uses a rich symbolic vocabulary: beasts, gemstones, stars, rivers, mountains, and sounds all play their part, but among all these natural symbols, numbers are given a very prominent place, both when they are mentioned explicitly (as in the dimensions of the New

Jerusalem, or the number of the Beast), and when they serve as a hidden way of organising the text (seven visions, seven bowls, etc.). But what did these numbers mean to the author?

The number seven is particularly rich in significance, being linked to the seven days of creation, which in the Old Testament writings was closely associated with the whole theme of the divine Covenant. In fact the Hebrew word for swearing an oath (*shava*), and making a covenant, is the verb form of the word for seven (*sheva*). The seventh day of creation therefore represents God's great oath of binding, an oath that seals the covenant of creation with a "nuptial" day of rest. The Seer of Patmos picks up on this theme and uses patterns of seven all through his book to suggest that we are seeing the end-point and goal of the Jewish Covenant and the final days of creation.

Another number he uses a great deal is twelve, which is associated in the Old Testament with the Tribes of Israel and in the New with the Apostles. There are also ancient astrological associations with the number twelve, since each of the Tribes was associated with a particular sign of the zodiac. Thus John is able once again to use the number to suggest the perfection in Christ both of the ancient Jewish religion *and* of the vast cosmos itself, all of which is reflected and transfigured in his final vision of the perfect City.

The following is a summary of the main numbers we will encounter in reading the Book of Revelation.

Key to the main symbolic numbers employed in Revelation

1	Unity, the First and Last
½	Limited time, i.e. time divided or fragmented
2	Division, symmetry, balance, two natures of Christ
3	The divine Trinity, a return to unity, the primordial relationship
3½	Imperfection, a time of trial (=7÷2)
4	The earth, the universe, dimensions of the material cosmos
6	The sum and product of 1, 2, 3; the days of creation
7	Earth joined to God (=4+3), perfection, God's sabbath "rest"
10	Authority (e.g. Commandments), or else simply a limited number (by contrast with 1000)
12	Tribes, Patriarchs, Apostles; 4x3 = the celestial order
666	The numerical equivalent of the name "Nero Caesar"
1000	Simply a very large number, or unlimited time
1260	The days equivalent to 3½ years (42 months of 30 days)
144,000	12 x 12 x 1000 (unlimited extension of the Tribes and Apostles)

The Theology of the Book of Revelation

Theologically speaking, the message of Revelation is the same as that of the Fourth Gospel. Its author believed in the divinity of Christ, and in the Trinity of God.

The doctrine of the Trinity may not have been worked out theologically yet, but the man who wrote this book was clearly a Trinitarian thinker. This is brought out strongly in Richard Bauckham's book, *The Theology of the Book of Revelation*. John's "Lamb" shares in divinity, but is never portrayed as a separate object of worship. Father and Son, therefore, are one God. As for the third divine Person, Revelation contains a total of fourteen references to the Holy Spirit. Significantly enough, these are divided into seven occurrences in the phrase "what the Spirit is saying to the Churches," and seven elsewhere. There are also exactly four references in the book to the "seven spirits" (or the sevenfold Spirit), each in association with the victory of the Lamb. This number, too, is significant. In John's symbolic language, fourfoldness represents the full extent of the world in its traditional "four directions," and is often found in combination with seven. At the end of Revelation, the oneness of the sevenfold Spirit is reaffirmed: "The Spirit and the Bride say, Come!"

John's *Apocalypse* may appear to be nothing but a kaleidoscope of bizarre images, but it has been extremely carefully constructed to express the meaning in human, historical and spiritual terms of the Revelation of Jesus

Christ. Experts have shown that this care extends even to the details of grammatical construction, and the numbers of times certain words and titles are used. We can be confident that the Holy Spirit is speaking through the human author of this wonderful text, and join our prayer to his as we say at the end, "Amen. Come, Lord Jesus!"

Part One (*Rv* 1:1 to 11:19)

So, with all this in mind, let us work through the text in a bit more detail.

In the first three chapters, John has a vision of Jesus Christ, who gives him messages for the seven churches of Asia Minor. In the next two chapters, John has a vision of heaven, and of a book in God's hand sealed with seven seals that only the Lamb (Jesus) is worthy to open. The Lamb proceeds to open the first six seals on the book. The opening of the seventh seal leads to the blowing of seven trumpets. The events associated with the first six trumpets take up the next two chapters. In the final two chapters of this Part, John is given a "little scroll" to eat, he is instructed to measure the temple, he is told of two martyrs who will serve as heavenly "witnesses", and at last the *seventh trumpet* is blown, signifying the final integration of heaven and earth: "The kingdom of the world has become the kingdom of our Lord and of his Christ" (11:15).

Seven messages, seven seals, and seven trumpets, and we are still only half way through Revelation! But at least we can say that the progression in the first Part is clear. Jesus has led John through a series of frames. First he steps through a door into heaven. Once there he sees a book. *Entering into the book* is the second stage in the journey. The opening of the seven seals can be seen as his journey into the book, as though each seal marked a new layer of depth. With the opening of the seventh seal, another series of visions begins. This is signified by the series of seven trumpets, ending with the "marriage of heaven and earth" that brings Part One to an end.

As for what is going on here, there are of course many interpretations. Some commentators see the whole Book of Revelation as a commentary on the early Christian liturgy, intended to be read aloud in the Christian assembly. Through the Seer's eyes we glimpse the inner meaning of salvation history, the Covenant with Israel, the (first) coming of Christ, and the persecutions of the Church, and we look forward to Christ's second coming. Our earthly Mass is seen as a cosmic liturgy in which the whole creation, men, angels and creatures of every kind, join in praise of the One who is worthy of all "blessing and glory and wisdom and thanksgiving and honour and power and might ... for every and ever" (*Rv* 7:12).

Inaugural vision and seven messages

Let us go through this first Part in more detail. First, John is told to write to the churches about what he sees: "what is and what is to take place hereafter" (1:19). In other words, he is to reveal to the young Christian communities the *meaning and goal of history*. In a sense, the whole Book of Revelation is this "letter to the churches," but in chapters 2 and 3 John presents a series of condensed messages, describing the tests and temptations that each of the seven churches must undergo as they struggle to remain faithful to the sacramental life of the Church. God is confronting the sins of the Christian community and offering to heal them with his mercy. In these messages are contained glimpses of the imagery and prophecies that will be expanded upon in the rest of the Book.

The fact that there are exactly seven churches is, of course, no coincidence. As mentioned, for John the number seven represents completeness, and these communities are taken as representing the full spectrum of Christian experience in the world. In fact, we can turn these messages into a spiritual exercise by applying them to ourselves. We can read them as an examination of conscience, as if in preparation for the sacrament of Confession. (The message to Ephesus cues us to do so, with its call to repentance.) We need to compare how we are now with the way we were when we first felt the impact of divine grace, when with Adam we walked with God among the trees in the garden.

The fourfold structure of the message to Ephesus is replicated in all those that follow. It begins (1) with a characterisation of the one from whom the message comes, in this case, *The words of him who holds the seven stars in his right hand, who walks among the seven golden lampstands.* Immediately after this comes (2) a description of the spiritual state of the church in question, and this is followed (3) by a promise. The closing remarks (4), as in each message, include the formula, *He who has an ear, let him hear what the Spirit says to the churches.*

The series of promises is very carefully constructed to reach its culmination in the letter to Laodicea with the promise of a place on the throne of God (equivalent to divinization by grace). This in turn prepares the ground for the vision John now receives, only three verses later; namely a revelation of the heavenly throne itself (4:2), the very centre of heavenly worship. The Christian approaches this throne with amazement and awe, and with the staggering promise that he will one day sit upon it himself, in the most intimate friendship with the One who reigns there resplendent "like jasper and carnelian" at the heart of a gigantic rainbow.

Throne vision and the seven seals of the Lamb's scroll

In chapter 4 John sees a door in heaven, and through it the throne of God surrounded by lesser thrones for twenty-four elders, seven torches representing the sevenfold Spirit of God, a sea of glass, and four living creatures full of eyes in the forms of lion, calf or bullock, man, and eagle, each with six wings, each praising the Trinity (cf. *Ezk* 1:10; *Is* 6:2-3). As they sing their praises, the elders cast down their crowns and join in. The vision is of a heavenly liturgy, an eternal act of adoration and worship. John seems to be saying that *liturgy*, after all, is what heaven *is*.

In chapter 5, John is shown a scroll sealed with seven seals, and weeps because there is no one worthy to open and read it. Then a Lamb appears, standing but slain, with its seven horns and seven eyes representing the sevenfold Spirit of God. (To us, a lamb with seven horns and eyes might seem a rather grotesque image, if we can visualise it at all. John is using a symbolic language in which horns represent power and eyes spiritual knowledge.) The Lamb is worthy to open the scroll. In the allocution already cited, Pope Benedict comments on this image of the Lamb "standing as if slain" as follows:

> On this earth, Jesus, the Son of God, is a defenceless, wounded and dead Lamb. Yet he stands up straight, on his feet, before God's throne and shares in the divine power. He has the history of the world in his hands. Thus, the Seer wants to tell us: trust in Jesus, do not be afraid of the opposing powers, of persecution! The wounded and dead Lamb is victorious! Follow the Lamb Jesus, entrust yourselves to Jesus, take his path! Even if in this world he is only

a Lamb who appears weak, it is he who triumphs!...

History remains indecipherable, incomprehensible. No one can read it. Perhaps John's weeping before the mystery of a history so obscure expresses the Asian Churches' dismay at God's silence in the face of the persecutions to which they were exposed at that time. It is a dismay that can clearly mirror our consternation in the face of the serious difficulties, misunderstandings and hostility that the Church also suffers today in various parts of the world.

John's vision of the "liturgy of heaven" continues with a reading of the Holy Scriptures, for as every creature in heaven and earth, under the earth and in the sea, along with the millions of angels, joins in with the praise of God (cf. *Heb* 12:22-4), the scroll is opened by the Lamb, just as the priest representing Christ interprets the readings in the earthly liturgy of the Christian community.

In chapter 6 we see the result of the opening of the seals in a series of visions. A white horse carries a crowned rider, perhaps representing the false messiah (the real one will appear in chapter 19), a red horse brings War, a black horse brings Judgment, a pale green horse brings Death. After the four horsemen are released from the first four seals, the fifth seal reveals the souls of the martyrs crying out for justice from under the altar, and the sixth the ending of the cosmic order in earthquake and star-fall. (These are the *unavoidable disasters* of which Jesus speaks in the Gospels: *Mt* 24, *Mk* 13, *Lk* 21.)

The opening of the seventh seal is preceded by an interlude in chapter 7, beginning with the four angels at the corners of the earth restraining the winds from the earth, sea, and trees, and with the dawn angel coming to seal 12,000 of the saved from each of the twelve tribes, making 144,000 in all. Then an even greater multitude of the saved, a multitude beyond count (those from outside the twelve Tribes?), washed white in the blood of the Lamb who has died for all, are also seen to be involved in the cosmic liturgy.

When the seal is finally opened there is silence in heaven "for about half an hour," following which trumpets are given to the "seven angels who stand before God" (8:1-2). These angels are the Archangels, of whom the canonical Scriptures only name three: Michael, Gabriel, and Raphael. Why the silence? Opening the final seal is like entering the eye of the whirlwind, the still centre around which everything turns. One series of dramatic visions has reached its climax, now we wait for something else to begin.

Seven trumpets

Each of the seven trumpets that are now sounded, beginning at Rv 8:7, announces a disaster that will befall the world outside the community of the saved, until the seventh, which is delayed. The first four trumpets mark the destruction of one third of the cosmos, grouped according to the third, fifth, and fourth days of creation respectively: earth and foliage (8:7), oceans (8:8-9), rivers and waters (8:10-11), sun, moon, and stars (8:12-13). The next two trumpets afflict those men "who have not the seal of God" with torment and with death, but fail to arouse repentance (9:20).

An angel "wrapped in a cloud, with a rainbow over his head", prophesying "no more delay" (10:1-7), now gives John a little scroll to eat, sweet to taste and bitter in the stomach, recalling the scroll eaten by the prophet Ezekiel (*Ezk* 2:8-3:3), and the Eucharist we receive at Mass. This contains the next set of prophecies he must deliver to the churches. If "we are what we eat," John must *become the book*: he must assimilate and become God's word.

The immediate result of John's eating the little scroll is another visionary experience, in which he glimpses what will be unfolded in more detailed visions later, concerning the war with the Beast. He is given a measuring rod like a sceptre (*Rv* 11:1) and told, again very like Ezekiel before him, to measure the Temple and those who worship there. ("Measuring" in the prophetic tradition usually represents a sign of divine protection.) The city will be trampled by the nations for 42 months, and the witnesses, who are also called "olive trees" and "lampstands" (here probably prophets in the spirit of Moses and Elijah) will prophesy for 1260 days, before the Beast kills them, but they will revive 3½ days later to ascend to heaven.

The eating of the little scroll and the conclusion of the trumpet section marks the mid-point of the book. From this section we have a view that enfolds both what came before and what will follow. It culminates with the blowing of the trumpet (the "last trump"), and the announcement that "The kingdom of the world has become the kingdom of our Lord and of his Christ, and he shall reign for ever and ever" (*Rv* 11:15). The twenty-four elders fall on their faces before God, the heavenly Temple is opened, and the Ark of the Covenant revealed within it (all this echoes the beginning of the "Liturgy of the Word" in Chapter 5, with the vision of the throne and the presentation of the seven-sealed scroll, although then the Ark was not revealed).

Part Two (*Rv* 12:1 to 22:21)

The second Part of Revelation begins with (you guessed it!) another series of seven visions. In chapter 12 we see a "great sign" in heaven: a Woman clothed with the sun, crowned with twelve stars, standing on the moon, giving birth in agony. Standing before her is a second "sign", a red Dragon with seven crowned heads, each with ten horns. He is waiting to devour the child, but the child when born is caught up to the throne of God, the Woman flees to the wilderness, where she is protected by God, and the Dragon, having been thrown down to earth by Michael and his angels, has to content himself with making war on the rest of her offspring. In chapter 13 he is joined by a Beast rising from the sea and a Beast from the earth.

The woman clothed with the sun is Mary, but also the Church founded by Christ (of which Mary is the first member). The Dragon and the two Beasts (the evil echo of the two heavenly witnesses introduced earlier in the book) portray an "Anti-Trinity": the Dragon as the Anti-Father, the Beast from the sea as the Anti-Logos or Anti-Christ, and the Beast from the earth as the Anti-Spirit. The two Beasts are generally agreed to represent the power of Rome and worldly authority in general, with which the Christian Church has to contend - in other words, those earthly powers that set themselves up as idols against God and his Christ. We could think of them as political and economic power respectively, since the second Beast causes people to be marked on the right hand or forehead with the name or number of the first (666) if they are to be able to buy or sell.

The child who is caught up to God's throne is Jesus. In the period between his Ascension to the throne of his Father, and his glorious return, the Christians who are the offspring of the Church will experience persecution from the Dragon and his agents on earth. But the purpose of the book is to reassure us that this time of persecution is short and not to be feared, for God will triumph. As Pope Benedict writes in his commentary, "suffering itself is already mysteriously mingled with the joy that flows from hope."

The fourth or central vision of this little series of seven comes in Chapter 14. It shows us the Lamb and his 144,000 followers on Mount Zion. Note that this time they are standing not in heaven but in a place midway between heaven and earth, with the "sound of many waters" suggesting baptism, therefore again the presence of the Church - and we also see in this "midheaven" three priestly angels proclaiming the Gospel and the fall of the Beast.

A fifth and sixth vision starting at 14:14 then show us four more angels (making a total of seven in this chapter), two of whom carry sickles with which they harvest and reap the earth at the command of the other two. God is telling us that nothing of value will be lost. The reaping and the pressing of the wine may be painful and bloody, but in this way all good things and people will be gathered safely into God's barns. Finally the seventh vision brings the series to an end with the Song of Moses and of the Lamb, marking a new Exodus, sung by those who had conquered the Beast, standing beside the sea of glass (15:2-4).

Seven bowl-plagues

Now "the temple of the tent of witness in heaven was opened, and out of the temple came the seven angels with the seven plagues, robed in pure bright linen, and with golden sashes across their chests" (15:5-6). The impression of a liturgical celebration is unavoidable, even if we don't normally think of the communication of disease as a liturgical act! God's justice and mercy poured out in blessing upon the good, rescuing them from evil, is experienced by their oppressors and by those given over to sin as a series of terrible punishments. It seems appropriate to think of these as the seven results of denying and rejecting the love of God present in the sacramental mysteries of the Church. Thus the pouring of the seven bowls (handed to the Archangels by the Cherubim at 15:7) results in plagues and disasters that repeat those associated with the seven scrolls in the parallel passages in chapters 4 to 7 and with the first six trumpets in chapters 8 and 9: they represent the "judgment" of God on sinful humanity (16:5,7). They remind us, too, of the plagues that Moses unleashed on the Egyptians - and to confirm this the Song of Moses (celebrating the crossing of the Red Sea and the escape from the Egyptians) is invoked at the beginning of the chapter.

The seventh bowl involves a triple catastrophe for the cities of men: "The great city was split into three parts, and the cities of the nations fell, and God remembered great Babylon, to make her drain the cup of the fury of his wrath' (16:19). Thus the seventh bowl introduces the extended vision in chapters 17, 18, and the first part of 19, of the fate of the "Great Whore," who is Babylon, the City of Sin, and the Beast on which she is seated. These are thrown down, in a catastrophic judgment lamented by the kings of the earth and celebrated in heaven. Babylon has to be completely destroyed if the new City, the City of God, is to descend from heaven. It must be rooted out from every soul, and we must be made to feel the anguish of that separation: "Alas, alas, for the great city that was clothed in fine linen, in purple and scarlet, adorned with gold, with jewels, and with pearls!" The culminating scene of rejoicing (19:1-10) echoes the opening of the "seven seals" section in Chapter 7.

It is worth noting that the seven bowl-plagues complete a series of three divine judgments said to issue from the throne-room of God: the seals, the trumpets, and the bowls. As Richard Bauckham points out, in each case the seventh member of the series portrays the arrival of God's kingdom, but the three series overlap: "the seventh seal-opening includes the seven trumpets and the seventh trumpet includes the seven bowls." Thus each series reaches the same goal, but "from a starting point progressively closer to the end." This helps to explain why the three series are also of increasing severity: the seal-openings affect a quarter of the earth, the trumpets a third, while the bowls affect everything.

Seven final visions of the Church

Finally, John sees heaven opened and the Word of God riding to war to defeat the Beast and its armies. The Dragon is bound for a thousand years before being cast into the fire, the dead are judged and book of life opened, and a new heaven and a new earth revealed. The Book of Revelation now moves from considering what will happen in history, during the time of the Church's struggle and persecution on earth, to what will happen "after" history.

The "holy city, new Jerusalem" comes down out of heaven from God, "prepared as a bride adorned for her husband" (*Rv* 21:2), contrasting vividly with the whore Babylon described earlier. Here the poetry of John's book is at its most moving, and its most consoling. "God himself will be with them; he will wipe away every tear from their eyes, and death shall be no more, neither shall there be mourning nor crying nor pain any more, for the former things have passed away" (21:3-4).

The streets of the city are paved with gold, but it is gold that is "transparent as glass." In the centre of the City is the "throne of God and of the Lamb," from which flows the river of the water of life "through the middle of the street." At the centre also, on both sides of the river, is the "tree of life" with its twelve fruitings and its leaves for the healing of the nations (cf. *Ezk* 47:12).

Visions of Heaven

The grand vision of heaven that immediately follows the seven messages to the churches of Asia is one of a series of such visions that punctuate the Book of Revelation. It is these I now want to go back and examine in more detail. These "stations" in John's journey offer us another way into the heart of his message. They show us the beauty, the divine glory, that calls us towards our destiny - the "light at the end of the tunnel" as it were. The Book of Revelation is not all doom and gloom! For that reason, in the sequence below I will concentrate on these stations that mark the stages of John's inner journey, skipping over the passages that separate them.

The First Vision of Heaven (1:12-20): **Christ**

John hears a voice like a trumpet, and "turns to see the voice" (*Rv* 1:12). The "voice" that he sees is the resurrected Christ, who resembles a "Son of man" (*Dn* 7:13). He is standing in the midst of seven golden lampstands: a *menorah* with seven branches for the seven days of creation. Each lamp on the stand represents one of the churches.

John's first and immediate vision, therefore, is not of the divine throne, but of Christ, who becomes his point of entry into the mysteries. It is by being with and in Christ, as every baptised Christian is with and in Christ, that the author of Revelation hears and sees all that is to follow. And the first thing that is given to him are the seven messages we have just examined in some detail.

The Second Vision of Heaven (4:1 to 5:14): **Trinity**

In chapter 4, after receiving the messages, John sees an open door in heaven, and the same Voice that he heard at the beginning calls him through it in the Spirit to see "what must take place." But he is not shown the future, as one might expect; he is given a glimpse of Eternity. He sees a throne on a crystal sea, crackling all around with lightning, surrounded by Four Creatures full of eyes and continually singing. Each possesses three pairs of wings, indicating their ability to move freely throughout the three worlds. The One seated on the Throne (not Christ but the Father) shines like the precious stones jasper and carnelian, white and red, and is surrounded by a rainbow described as being "like an emerald."

Corresponding to the seven stars which John saw in the hand of the Son in the first vision, which were there called the "angels of the churches," he now sees seven torches burning before the Throne, described as the "seven spirits of God." We can think of them as aspects of the one Holy Spirit, and also as the Spirit manifested in the seven days of creation (the opening of the Book of Genesis is never far away for John).

The twenty-four Elders seated around the One on the Throne represent the assembled patriarchs of Old and New Testament, but also the powers of heaven, the governors of the cosmos. In response to the song of the Four, they are continually throwing themselves down and casting their crowns before the Father. This signifies that the supreme power of God is not imposed by force upon creation, but is given to him willingly; he rules by love not fear.

The whole image, startlingly intense, resembles an oriental *mandala*. The One seated on the Throne is portrayed in two shining colours, surrounded by a third colour (green) at the centre of the rainbow, with seven torches, encircled in turn by the Four Creatures (covered in eyes and wings), and the twenty-four Elders (dressed in white and gold). But the image is not a static tableau, for it is full of overwhelming sounds and dynamic movement, of song and voices and thunder.

The vision of the Father is now followed by a vision of the Son. The Father holds a sealed scroll that no one else is worthy to open. John weeps at this, feeling so intensely on behalf of the whole creation the need for the scroll to be opened. The Lion-who-is-the-Lamb is in the "midst" of the Throne, with seven rays of light and the seven spirits upon him. The Lamb takes the scroll, whereupon the Creatures and the Elders sing "a new song," the song of the Redeemer.

Whereas the first song, to the Father (*Rv* 4:11), began, "Worthy are you...for you created all things," the new song, accompanied now by the harps and incense of a heavenly liturgy representing the prayers of the saints, begins, "Worthy are you to take the scroll and open its seals, for you were slain and by your blood you ransomed men for God..."; and every creature in heaven and earth and under the earth and in the sea, together with the millions of angels, joins in the praise, for the world that was created by the Father has been redeemed, united with God in the Spirit through the Lamb's eternal sacrifice.

The Third Vision of Heaven (7:9 to 8:5): **Church**

The first vision had been a vision of Christ in his earthly though transfigured form. Through him John was given a second vision, a vision of the Father, and of the Trinity and cosmos in spiritual unison. This vision now continues and is extended into the third, for the opening of the seals takes place in heaven, even if we also see its impact on the earth. We are standing with John in heaven, on the plane of consciousness represented by the glassy sea, the sea of the "upper waters" (*Gn* 1:7). What he sees now, after the opening of the first six seals, is a vision of the Church, of the 144,000 descended from Israel and an

unnumbered multitude from every other nation who have
come out of the "great tribulation."

Whether or not this "tribulation" refers to an historical
persecution, such as the one that may have taken place in
John's lifetime under the Emperor Nero ("666"),
symbolically it may be taken to represent the trials of life
in the fallen world, and at the hands of evil men, from
which the Lamb has rescued us. Those who have washed
their clothes "white in the blood of the Lamb" (*Rv* 7:14)
have received baptism, for indeed "all of us who have
been baptised into Christ Jesus were baptised into his
death" (*Rm* 6:3). And the heavenly Elder who is speaking
to John (perhaps the spiritual counterpart of John himself)
describes their situation (*Rv* 7:16-17) in what amounts to
a summary of the Sermon on the Mount that
simultaneously looks forward to the vision of the New
Jerusalem at the end of the whole book:

> They shall hunger no more, neither thirst any more;
> the sun shall not strike them, nor any scorching heat.
> For the Lamb in the midst of the throne will be their
>   shepherd,
> and he will guide them to springs of living water;
> and God will wipe away every tear from their eyes.

In keeping with the fact that this is a vision of the Church,
the opening of the seventh seal is followed by an offering
of the prayers of the saints by angels standing at a golden

altar before the Throne, after which the seven trumpets are sounded.

The Fourth Vision of Heaven (11:15-19): ***Judgment***

During the sounding of the trumpets and the plagues that ensue, John's vantage-point shifts back to the earth. It is from there that he sees the mighty angel with "legs like pillars of fire" (*Rv* 10:1) holding the little scroll that is given him to eat. But after he has measured the temple and the altar on earth, and seen the two witnesses called up to heaven in a cloud, and when the seventh trumpet is sounded, John is given his fourth glimpse of heaven. The first vision was of Christ, the second of the Trinity, the third of the Church; the fourth in this logical series is of the Judgment. For the Elders chorus (*Rv* 11:17-18):

> We give thanks to you, Lord God Almighty,
> who are and who were,
> that you have taken your great power and begun to reign.
> The nations raged, but your wrath came,
> and the time for the dead to be judged,
> for rewarding your servants, the prophets and saints,
> and those who fear your name, both small and great,
> and for destroying the destroyers of the earth.

With this vision, something new is revealed in heaven: "God's temple in heaven was opened, and the ark of his covenant was seen within his temple." John has just been measuring the earthly temple (which, by the way, suggests to some that this text was written before the Romans destroyed it in AD 70); now he is shown the heart of the temple that is its archetype. But the vision of the Ark of the Covenant at once gives way to another vision of what is essentially the same thing under a different aspect: the Woman whose flesh carries within it the New Covenant of Jesus Christ. For now "a great sign appeared in heaven, a woman clothed with the sun, with the moon under her feet, and on her head a crown of twelve stars; she was with child and she cried out in her pangs of birth, in anguish for delivery" (*Rv* 12:1-2).

As explained earlier, we have now moved from what I am calling Part One of the book into Part Two. The adventure of the Woman, the Dragon, and the two Beasts that unfolds in the succeeding chapters is the story of the Covenant and the Anti-Trinity. But it is also the story of the creation, and of the fallen angels, and of their long battle with God. The Woman is the personification of the whole created order "full of grace" (clothed with the sun). The child with whom she is pregnant is the light that darkness cannot overcome (*Jn* 1:5). The second sign that appears in heaven in this vision is the spirit of evil: a red Dragon with seven heads (opposed to the sevenfold Spirit of God). Having failed to devour the child in heaven (because he is immediately taken up to God's throne), the Dragon is thrown down to the earth by Michael. There, with the Child now out of reach, he seeks to sweep the woman away in a flood of water. But "the earth came to the help of the woman," by swallowing the flood, so his third ploy is to make war on the Church: "the rest of her offspring, on those who keep the commandments of God and bear testimony to Jesus" (*Rv* 12:17) - meaning the good Jews and Christians. This he does by means of the Beasts from the sea and the earth.

The Fifth Vision of Heaven (14:1-13): **Harvest**

At the beginning of chapter 14, the tale of the two Beasts is interrupted by the fifth vision of heaven, which is like a reprise of the third, the vision of the Church, for it concerns once more the 144,000 who are singing the "new song" of the Redeemer. But in each successive vision, there are important variations, or some new element is added, and this time the Lamb and the 144,000 are standing on Mount Zion, and we are told that the seal on their foreheads includes the name of the Lamb and of the Father. In other words, these are the formally baptised, seen in this state of spiritual consciousness. But where is Mount Zion? Meister Eckhart comments here: "Now John says he saw a lamb standing on the mountain. I say John was himself the mountain on which he saw the lamb. And whoever wants to see the lamb of God must himself be the mountain, and ascend into his highest and purest part."[1]

There are also three angels proclaiming the Gospel, and the voice of the Holy Spirit is heard directly: a voice from heaven tells John to write the Beatitude, "Blessed are the dead who from now on die in the Lord," and the Spirit responds, "Blessed indeed, that they may rest from their labours, for their deeds follow them" (*Rv* 14:13). The voice of the Spirit is "like the sound of many waters and like the sound of thunder," it is "like the sound of harpists playing on their harps, and they sing a new song before the throne" (*Rv* 14:2-3) - musical, then, but on a scale and with an intensity that human words cannot adequately describe. Francesca Murphy comments on the significance of the fact that the voice sounds like waters (as also when it is the voice of Christ in 1:15):

> Water and Spirit come together in the actions of creation and baptism: this is the aspect of God which brings about *relation*. Water is a sign of a communication which is not just a transfer of information from one ego to another, but a flowing exchange of self. Coming out of the water is the moment of liberation, the birth of the person. When John's attention is drawn to the Lamb who holds the book and feels all around him voices like the booming of the sea, he is immersed in something wild and primeval, but also in a medium of communication, which transforms his understanding.[2]

Christ has led John into the heart of the Trinity and shown him the Church in her heavenly and universal form, the "Church Triumphant." Now he is to see the Church on her way to that final state through the suffering that measures our distance from heaven: "the earth was reaped" (*Rv* 14:16), and "the wine press was trodden outside the city, and blood flowed from the wine press, as high as a horse's bridle, for 1600 *stadia*" (*Rv* 14:20). The very specific figure of 1600 mentioned here is the square of 40 - a number associated with Noah's flood, representing also the tenfold multiplication of the four directions of space. The world is submerged not in water this time but in blood (albeit only "as high as a horse's bridle"!); that is, in human life poured out before the throne of God, blood becoming wine.

The Sixth Vision of Heaven (Rv 15): **Purification**

In the sixth vision John sees the sea of glass again, but now it is mingled with fire (*Rv* 15:2). The "temple of the tent of witness in heaven" is opened, and the seven last plagues are sent forth: the bowls or vials of wrath. They are the last plagues, the final purification of the earth before the new can be revealed.

The Seventh Vision of Heaven (19:1-10): **Invitation**

In heaven John hears and sees the celebration that ensues when the harlot city is cast down, in three great hymns, a triple Hallelujah, the third of which introduces a new theme: "Let us rejoice and exult and give him the glory, for the marriage of the Lamb has come, and his Bride has made herself ready" (*Rv* 19:7). The angel tells John, "Blessed are those who are invited to the marriage supper of the Lamb."

By this point it is admittedly becoming hard to distinguish one vision of heaven from another, for the visions succeed one another so quickly, and the actions of the angels are interwoven with the drama being enacted on earth. (In fact, as I mentioned earlier, Ian Boxall distinguishes seven separate visions of the Church just between 19:11 and 22:11.) The Word of God rides forth on his white horse, with his armies (*Rv* 19:11-16), for the last battle, and the "supper of God" which sounded so charming in the previous verses is revealed to be a meal made of the "flesh of kings…the flesh of all men, both free and slave, both small and great" (*Rv* 19:18). In this war the Dragon is finally defeated, and with his two Beasts is thrown into the lake of fire and brimstone, to be tormented for ever.[3]

Now John sees "a great white throne and him who sat upon it; from his presence earth and sky fled away, and no place was found for them" (*Rv* 20:11). The book of life is opened, the dead are judged, and Death and Hades themselves are thrown into the lake of fire.

The Eighth Vision of Heaven (21:1 to 22:5):
New Heaven and Earth

The final two chapters of Revelation are of a radically different tone and mood than the others. It is impossible not to note the transformation in mood and atmosphere. All the turmoil and conflict of the Judgment and Purification of the earth has been resolved and overcome: the storm in the night is over, and a new day is dawning, the eighth day of creation. These verses reveal the ultimate effect John's visions were aiming at, and the change in consciousness they were designed to bring about. With each successive heavenly vision in this series, the integration of heaven and earth comes closer, and now it has been achieved.

The Second Coming of Jesus Christ

Then he said to them, "Nation will rise against
nation, and kingdom against kingdom; there will be
great earthquakes, and in various places famines
and pestilences... And there will be signs in sun and
moon and stars, and upon the earth distress of
nations in perplexity at the roaring of the sea and
the waves, men fainting with fear and with
foreboding of what is coming on the world; for the
powers of the heavens will be shaken. And then they
will see the Son of man coming in a cloud with
power and great glory."

Lk 21:10-11, 25-8

We have already seen that the second half of the Book of
Revelation is particularly concerned with the Second
Coming, the coming in glory of the God-Man. That
"glory" is ultimately the serene splendour of the Holy City
itself, the descent of which is itself an image of the Second
Coming. But before this final resolution is achieved, the
descent of the Logos provokes a war throughout the
cosmos. It is as though all evil, in order to be eliminated,
must first be flushed out from hiding, and confronted head

on. The details of this process concern us intimately, and therefore it is important to give them some attention in this chapter - along with the whole problematic of evil, and of God's relationship to a suffering world.

The horrors described in Revelation are not at all at odds with the Gospels, as we can see from the passages in Luke, just quoted, and Jesus's extended prophecies concerning the fall of Jerusalem and the "close of the age" as recorded in Matthew 24 and 25.

When time is unmasked by the eternal, nothing is safe. The prophetic eye measures the distance between earth and heaven, and the violence of these apocalyptic scenes reflects the greatness of this distance, the intensity of the contrast, when the one is brought kicking and screaming into the light of the other. In order to understand what is meant by the Second Coming, we must let the images speak. *All that you know is at an end*.

Monsters from the Pit

Even CGI [computer-generated imagery] would find it hard to cope with some of the monsters John evokes:

> In appearance the locusts were like horses arrayed for battle; on their heads were what looked like crowns of gold; their faces were like human faces, their hair like women's hair, and their teeth like lions' teeth; they had scales like iron breastplates, and the noise of

their wings was like the noise of many chariots with horses rushing into battle. They have tails like scorpions, and stings, and their power of hurting men for five months lies in their tails (*Rv* 9:7-10).

These particular monsters from the Pit are associated with the "first woe," that of the fifth trumpet, which afflicts those who do not wear the seal of God upon their forehead. Though in the form of locusts, they are given the command not to hurt "the grass of the earth or any green growth or any tree" (9:4). The next to be released (by the sixth trumpet) are four angels that had been bound at the Euphrates, with a cavalry of "two myriads of myriads" (200,000): "the riders wore breastplates the colour of fire and of sapphire and of sulphur, and the heads of the horses were like lions' heads, and fire and smoke and sulphur issued from their mouths" (9:17), although their power to kill lies also in their tails, which are like serpents.

Two armies of monsters, then, one from the Pit and one from the Euphrates, with the power to sting and wound and kill, but they can only affect those who have rejected God - and the time for repentance seems to be past, for none of those who survive these trials, it seems, will give up their idol worship or murdering or sorceries or thievery (9:20-21). Their afflictions are simply the natural consequence of attachment to sin, a refusal to be rescued from a fallen and collapsing world full of false and transient delights.

God's overlordship is clear: it is by divine command that the monsters are released, and they can only act within the limits he sets. Does this make him responsible for the suffering they inflict? He permits it, and does so for a purpose - to bring the whole world ultimately to the transformation glimpsed at the end of the book. When we commit evil we only see the beginning of a process, one that may appear pleasant enough. If we could see rightly we would see even in the beginning of the act its natural end, which is the torment it stores up for us, by virtue of its true nature, in the Pit. But even God cannot prevent us seeing this at last, if the process is to run its course. The result is either repentance or a hardening of the heart, and it is the hardened heart that we are concerned with here. This hardening is what permits the separation of the saved from the damned, who "shall be tormented with fire and brimstone in the presence of the holy angels and in the presence of the Lamb" (14:10), while the blessed "rest from their labours." Final impenitence makes the divine presence a torment.

The violence that takes place in Revelation simply reveals what has been lurking under the surface of things ever since the Fall. Like the suffering of Jesus on the Cross, it is intended to open our eyes to reality, the reality of sin. Once that has been done, and done definitively, we can each make our choice between life and death, and the harvest of the earth, now "fully ripe" (14:15), can be gathered in.

The Beastly Trinity

In Chapter 12, we are shown two great signs in heaven: the Woman and the Dragon, archetypes recognisable from every culture. Yet this is no serene image of majesty, not yet: the great Queen, though crowned with the stars of heaven (representing the Apostles, or the Tribes), is crying out in the pangs of birth, and the Dragon now stands before her like a horrific midwife, to devour her child. When the child is born, he is wrenched from her by God, and she for her part is cruelly separated from him by being sent into the wilderness. Yet this apparent harshness is really kind: the child, after all, is kept safe from the Dragon, and the woman nourished and protected.

If we identify the Woman with Mary (although she is also *Ecclesia*, the Church) these six verses can be said to sum up the advent of Christ: almost as soon as he is born (for that first thirty years must have gone by in a flash) he reaches his manhood and dies on the Cross, leaving his mother and the Church behind in the wilderness as he ascends to the Father. Yet the cycle of the Incarnation from conception to Ascension is only a prelude to the battle his coming provokes, which culminates in his eventual return. This battle begins in heaven, not on earth, as all things do. "Now war arose in heaven, Michael and his angels fighting against the dragon; and the dragon and his angels fought, but they were defeated and there was no longer any place for them in heaven. And the great dragon was thrown down..." (12:7-9). Being archetypal, the battle is contemporaneous with any point in time.

The serpent is cast down not into hell, but rather "to earth and sea" (12:12), to pursue the woman and, failing her, the Church. "And he stood on the sand of the sea" (12:18), linking earth and sea like the great angel of *Rv* 10:1-3, and from the two places where he stands arise the two beasts, the one with ten horns and seven heads, who is the demonic counterpart of God's Son, and the other with two horns like a lamb but speaking like a dragon (13:11), who is the Unholy Spirit, making men worship the first beast and bringing fire from heaven. Against the two beastly witnesses are ranged the two "olive trees" we encountered in chapter 11.

The overthrow of the evil kingdom is accomplished by the bowls or "Vials of Wrath" in chapter 16. The word for "wrath," *thymos*, means also "passion," and God's anger must always be understood as a manifestation of love - the same love that was poured out on the Cross. The seven bowls are tipped like a libation upon the earth, turning the waters to blood and scorching men with the heat of the sun. As I suggested, they correspond to the sacraments, outpourings of divine grace, here experienced as so many forms of torment by those who have rejected the love of God, and the last of them cleaves the Unholy City into three parts.

The Fall of Babylon the Great

In order to reach the new city, we must leave the old. We must detach ourselves from all that binds us to the world that is passing. The extended prophecies concerning Babylon, that form a central narrative in the second half of Revelation, remind me of Plato's myth about the fall of Atlantis, but also those detailed meditations on death and decay (sometimes conducted in a graveyard) that the Buddhist monk is enjoined to practice in order to detach himself from the world.

The narrative is anticipated at Revelation 14:8, when the second of the three angels who are summarising the message of Revelation as a whole says, "Fallen, fallen is Babylon the great, she who made all nations drink the wine of her impure passion." Then, after the harvesting and reaping, and the seven bowl-plagues, we return to a more detailed account of her fall in chapters 17 and 18.

The introduction to this fall is hard to interpret. The woman/city is seated on the scarlet beast with seven heads and ten horns, which signify (according to the angel who is John's guide at this point) seven hills, seven kings - five of whom have already fallen - and ten kings who are due to rule for an hour. I dare not venture into the thicket of interpretations that have grown up around these verses. It seems to be fairly certain that the seven hills are those of Rome. More interesting is the reference to the beast that "was, and is not, and is to ascend from the bottomless pit and go to perdition" (17:8). This is in deliberate counterpoint, repeated three times, to the three-times repeated title of God, "the One who is and who was and who is to come" (1:4, 1:8, 4:8). The ontological contrast between God and his opponent is clear: the latter belongs to the past, not the eternal present, and he is "coming" (from below) only to be judged and expunged.

In chapter 18 an angel with great authority and splendour repeats the earlier phrase, "Fallen, fallen is Babylon the great…"; perhaps it is the same angel, but God never seems to run out of these radiant beings as far as John is concerned. The extended meditation begins, and it takes the form of a dramatic dialogue or musical piece for several voices:

- the first angel (18:2-3);

- a voice from heaven that calls, "Come out of her, my people, lest you take part in her sins, lest you share in her plagues" (18:4-8);

- the kings of the earth weeping and wailing over the smoke of her burning (18:9-10);

- the merchants of the earth bewailing because "no one buys their cargo any more" (18:11-17), cargo listed in splendid detail;

- shipmasters and seafaring men (18:17-20);

- the angel who throws a millstone in the sea (18:21-24).

This music of several voices, beginning and ending in the angelic, then gives way to the song of the multitude in heaven, joined by the elders and living creatures before the throne.

The dialogue is important to read line by line, and preferably aloud, as John would have intended. We are meant to feel the charm of the great worldly city in our own hearts, for we are all tempted by her "fine linen, purple, silk and scarlet, all kinds of scented wood," gold, jewels, and pearls. If we are to "come out of her," it is this temptation we need to reject. We will be helped by the vision of an alternative: the heavenly city of John's final vision.

If we think the images quaint, just because they refer to spices and slaves and harpists and minstrels rather than restaurants and credit cards and CDs then we have missed the point. We are all implicated, we are all entangled in a way of life that will eventually come crashing down around us, like a great millstone in the sea. What happens next is up to us.

The Return of the Child

We last saw the child of the woman clothed with the sun, "one who is to rule all the nations with a rod of iron," being caught up to God and his throne at 12:5. Now he is fully grown, and he makes rather a dramatic entrance.

> Then I saw heaven opened, and behold, a white horse! He who sat upon it is called Faithful and True, and in righteousness he judges and makes

war. His eyes are like a flame of fire, and on his head are many diadems; and he has a name inscribed which no one knows but himself. He is clad in a robe dipped in blood, and the name by which he is called is The Word of God. And the armies of heaven, arrayed in fine linen, white and pure, followed him on white horses. From his mouth issues a sharp sword with which to smite the nations, and he will rule them with a rod of iron; he will tread the wine press of the fury of the wrath of God the Almighty (*Rv* 19:11-15).

We have been told that each person who conquers will receive a white stone, with a new name that no one else will know (*Rv* 2:17). This is a deep mystery, for as we see here it connects us with God himself, whose own name is also secret. Even "Logos" or "Word," by which Scripture refers to him, is not that name, but only the one by which others call him. As Pope Benedict writes in *Jesus of Nazareth*, "God's love for each individual is totally personal and includes this mystery of a uniqueness that cannot be divulged to other human beings." The interior dimension of the "I", where each of us is alone in the presence of God, is an essential part of our likeness to the Son, whose interior life is open only to the Father in the Spirit.

The coming of the White Rider causes the Beast and the kings of the earth with all their armies to gather in opposition, making war on God. Their final defeat is inevitable: "and all the birds were gorged with their flesh" (19:21).

How many of those will burn in hell? We cannot know, for the number of the saved, though relatively small (144,000) compared to the billions who have lived, is symbolic, and not intended to be taken literally. It might refer to billions. It might include everybody, according to some of the most influential theologians of the twentieth century - Karl Barth, Karl Rahner, Hans Urs von Balthasar. These came close to arguing for "universal salvation," believing that Christians may legitimately hope that in some sense hell would turn out, in the end, to be empty (at least of human beings). Others have argued that this would reduce much of Scripture, and many of the statements of Christ, to the status of threats that a grown-up uses to terrify children into good behaviour, and which he has no intention of carrying out. However, this does not follow. There may be a real possibility that I will walk over a cliff, even if I never do. To put it another way, God does not have to make sure that some people fall over the cliff in order to ensure that his warnings against walking too close to the edge do not remain an "empty threat."

To the extent we remain creatures in time, without having reached our final destination, we remain in peril. No doubt most of us are in much greater danger than we realise, since we do not take the state of our souls as seriously as we should, and our sense of sin has become numb. As a society, too, we are used to hiding our own cruelty under the carpet. We pride ourselves on being civilised, yet our wars are as brutal as any in history, millions of our children are exterminated in the womb, and the "abomination of desolation" has entered the souls of a whole generation.

Our spiritual peril is depicted graphically in the Book of Revelation. The Lord's return signifies a restoration of order both in the world and in our souls that must come, if the will of God is to be done "on earth as it is in heaven." But while the Apocalypse reveals what has become of us, and the perils that face us, it also gives us a choice. We do not have to sink with Babylon. There is another place to go. John tells us that nothing unclean will enter into that shining City to stain its radiance, and beyond the horizon presented by an everlasting torment of fire and brimstone (20:10) there is a moment when Death and Hades themselves will be thrown into the lake of fire (20:14). The unclean elements of the old world, with all that pertains exclusively to the old order, including death, will be cast off like slag, and dissolve like dreams as the dawn rises.

The New Jerusalem

Then I saw a new heaven and a new earth; for the first heaven and the first earth had passed away, and the sea was no more. And I saw the holy city, Jerusalem, coming down out of heaven from God, prepared as a bride adorned for her husband; and I heard a great voice from the throne saying, 'Behold, the dwelling of God is with men. He will dwell with them, and they shall be his people, and God himself will be with them; he will wipe away every tear from their eyes, and death shall be no more, neither shall there be mourning nor crying nor pain any more, for the former things have passed away.

Rv 21:1-4

Entry to the City is by way of twelve whole pearls that form the gates of the Tribes. Symbolically, it is easy to see why the gates should be pearls. A pearl is a living jewel formed around some impurity that has entered under the oyster's shell, and so can represent sufferings endured and transformed. One meaning of this is surely that it is through the suffering of the children of Israel (the twelve tribes) that mankind will enter the City. But the image applies individually, as well as collectively. Each of us must transform our own impurity into its opposite, for "nothing unclean" can enter the City (21:27), and only the pure in heart will see God (*Mt* 5:8).

The jewels upon the city walls and its foundations incorporate the beauty of the stars into the adornment of the City, and the pearly gates the beauty of the moon. Within the walls, "the street of the city was pure gold, transparent as glass" (21:21). The sea of glass (4:6) mingled with fire (15:2) has become the golden crystal of the city street, as the warmth and glory of love has entered into and transmuted the substance on which it stands. Thus the City, which John describes as feminine, is the final form of the Woman clothed with the sun, standing on the moon, crowned with stars.

> *There shall no more be anything accursed, but the throne of God and of the Lamb shall be in it, and his servants shall worship him; they shall see his face, and his name shall be on their foreheads. And night shall be no more; they need no light of lamp or sun, for the Lord God will be their light, and they shall reign for ever and ever. (Rv 22:3-5; cf. Is 60:19-21.)*

This is a depiction of the final state of the world, but also of the mind of the Christian united with God. The state being described here - in which we see by the "light" that is God - is called the Beatific Vision. According to Saint Thomas, in this life we can only know things by the mediation of an idea in our mind (as it were by "reflected" light), but in the next we will know God directly, since the place of the idea in our mind is taken by the actual essence of God[4]. An inward light from God will make us shine without the need of lamp or sun, because only like can see like. So it is that "when he appears we shall be like him, for we shall see him as he is" (1 *Jn* 3:2). In that glorified state, to know is to be known, as bridegroom and bride: "Now I know in part; then I shall understand fully, even as I have been fully understood" (1 *Co* 13:12).

The Christian lives in the anticipation of the blissful Vision of God, but because he is a temporal creature the goal is not yet achieved. We do not yet experience the influx of the *lumen gloriae*; we are not yet incandescent. The infused virtue of faith must serve in the place of this light, for the time being. We know God but not by sight, rather by touch, like children in the dark holding their mother's hand. This is the characteristic of a Christian consciousness: a constant awareness of God as a presence behind the world, by the power of a faith that we know is flowing into us from beyond ourselves, which we might lose at any moment but for that very reason assures us that God is there. The authentic Christian consciousness is therefore marked by *joy* and *gratitude*, which are the twin fruits of the experience of being loved. Even when these are not consciously felt or adverted to, they remain as a kind of subconscious substance in our souls for as long as faith continues to be alive in us.

The joy, ecstasy, and serenity that we sense at the end of Revelation, in the final vision of the City, is precisely this, the fruit of a faith so intense that it has dissolved all but the last veil between ourselves and the throne of God.

Endnotes

[1] Sermon 24, in *Meister Eckhart: Sermons and Treatises*, Vol. I, 193.

[2] F. Murphy, *The Comedy of Revelation*, 216.

[3] The chronology here is hard to interpret, not doubt because it was not intended to be taken literally. It is said in chapter 20 that Satan will be bound for a thousand years while the martyrs reign with Christ in the "first resurrection," *before* the final judgment. This is probably most safely interpreted with Augustine as referring to the period of the Church on earth, in which the saints "reign" with Christ from the altar and in the liturgical calendar.

[4] See St Thomas Aquinas, *Summa Contra Gentiles*, Bk 3, Ch. 51.

Further Reading

Ian Boxall, *The Revelation of St John* (London: A. & C. Black, 2006)

Scott Hahn, *The Lamb's Supper: The Mass as Heaven on Earth* (New York: Doubleday, 1999)

Richard Bauckham, *The Theology of the Book of Revelation* (Cambridge University Press, 1993)

There are of course a large number of good commentaries and Study Bibles available, including *The CTS New Catholic Bible* (2007), which includes helpful introductions and notes.

Note

The text of this book is based on my forthcoming *Apocalypse: Unveiling the Christian Tradition Through the Book of Revelation* (SCM, 2008). I am grateful to the series editor Dr Conor Cunningham for permission to use parts of it here.